Survive and Thrive

Beginners Complete Guide to Off-Grid Living and Family Preparedness

Jim Kilpatrick

TRADITIONALLY
MODERN

Atlanta, Georgia USA

ISBN 978-1-49438-487-6

9 781494 384876 >

Words from Our Readers

"I always wanted to go off the grid, and perhaps this book has just showed me how. One of the best guides I've ever read."

★★★★★Elijah Mote, New York

"If you're someone who likes to be selfsufficient and in complete control of theirlives then you'll love this book. It gave me a lot of food for thought and ideas for a different way of life."

★★★★★Lynda Gibson, Ohio

"I wish I had this book in my possession ages ago. It would have saved me a lot of trouble and money. Well, better late than never."

★★★★★Frank Sullivan, Mansfield

Thank you for downloading my book. Please REVIEW this book. I need your feedback to make the next version better. Thank you so much!

MEMBER

AHHA

AMERICAN
HOLISTIC
HEALTH
ASSOCIATION

Books by Jim Kilpatrick

Beginner's Backyard Chickens

Survive and Thrive

Simple Food Storage Strategies

www.amazon.com/author/jimkilpatrick

Before You Start Reading

It may sound strange, but having some survival skills and more importantly being self-sufficient is at our times more important than ever. Natural catastrophes have become something very common and during the recent past we have witnessed more than a dreadful event when the wrath of nature has taken us by surprise.

People say that you can't be prepared for everything, but that doesn't mean that you shouldn't be prepared for anything. Going off the Grid may sound as a weird concept but, if you think about it, it no longer is. Being prepared to face a disaster doesn't make you a fatalist, it just makes you cautious, while the whole process of reaching a point of self-sufficiency can prove a fun and worthwhile experience as well.

All the whats, the hows and the whys of your journey are explained in detail in this guide. It tells you all about the land you should build your house on; it highlights the importance of keeping sufficient supplies of food and water; and it guarantees you a way out of power-cuts. Going off the grid, or even just getting to know how to do so, could someday save your life and the lives of your loved ones, and there's nothing more important than that.

Table of Contents

Disclaimer

While all attempts have been made to provide effective, verifiable information in this Book, neither the Author nor Publisher assumes any responsibility for errors, inaccuracies, or omissions. Any slights of people or organizations are unintentional.

Introduction

With modern technology, we've been introduced a lot of new conveniences—super-fast internet connections, cell phones, a ready supply of food and water, access to any supplies that we need . . . but we've also become dependent on those conveniences and the people and companies that supply them. Do you remember having to call a travel agent instead of just booking your flight and hotel online? What about getting a busy signal when you called someone's house from your home landline phone? These are things that people are rapidly forgetting as we've come to rely on some modern technological miracles.

Unfortunately, as many recent events have shown (think of the tsunami in Japan, or the wildfires in Colorado), depending on these suppliers always comes with a risk. If a natural disaster happens, or a military/political uprising takes place, or you just lose power in your part of the country (people living in southern California can attest to this being a very real possibility), you'll suddenly find yourself without all of the marvels that have made life in today's world so convenient. And most people have absolutely no idea what to do when that happens.

That's one reason that many people are moving off the grid and learning to meet their own needs, as well as their family's, without recourse to the suppliers of all the things I mentioned above. You never know when something catastrophic might happen, and being prepared can give you great peace of mind. That's not the only reason people are doing it, though—with the recent popularity of "green" living and eco-friendliness, people are starting to get more interested in living closer to nature, and in concert with the earth, instead of simply taking advantage of it. Some people don't like the idea of being dependent on power and water providers. Others just want a challenge.

Whatever the reason that you're interested in going off the grid, I applaud you, and I'm glad that you picked up this book! I'll be laying out all of the lessons that I've learned in my own time spent living self-sufficiently, and I'll be giving you advice on how to go about planning and executing your move off the grid. I've long been interested in gardening, woodwork, backyard farming, and other things like that, so moving myself, my wife, and my two teenagers off the grid seemed to be a logical extension of those interests and skills. I've gained quite a bit of experience in self-sufficient living over the past years, and I sincerely hope that the knowledge I've been able to put down in this book will help you with your shift.

With that said, I give you the rest of this book, and I wish you well in your preparations. Be patient, be resilient, and above all, have a lot of fun!

Jim Kilpatrick

1. What is Self-Sufficiency?

Before getting into the main part of the book, I think it's important to take a moment to talk about what living off the grid actually *means*. People throw around words like "off-grid" and "self-sufficiency," but not many people take the time to properly define them before they start talking about them. First, I'd like to make it clear what living self-sufficiently off the grid is *not*:

- It's not going back to the Stone Age. Most self-sufficient homesteaders enjoy many of the same modern luxuries that you do now.
- It's not "going underground." If you're running from the law and want to disappear, you're reading the wrong book.
- It doesn't require a large family (if you're picturing twelve children working on a farm, you might have the wrong idea).
- It doesn't mean giving up your entire social or professional life.
- It's not impossibly difficult.

Now that I've dispelled at least a couple potential misunderstandings, I can get to what off-grid living *is*:

- It's possible for anyone to do.
- It's living without dependence on public works and utilities.
- It's a great way to learn a huge number of useful skills.
- It's providing for yourself.
- It's a lot of fun!

I hope that you have a little better idea of what we're talking about here; you're going to have to give up some things and work harder on others, but you'll still have a lot of the advantages of modern living, if you choose to. You'll likely be living in a rural area, but you don't need to be totally secluded—you can drive into town or to see friends whenever you want, and you'll have enough electricity to host a party when you feel like it. A lot of people think that off-the-grid living is extremely rudimentary and primitive, but it doesn't have to be! Of course, if you want it to be, that's totally fine—but don't feel like you need to do it that way.

Being self-sufficient just means that you don't need to rely on utility companies or governmental services; you won't be paying an electricity or water bill, you won't need to rely on a supply of food from the grocery store, you won't be relying on public schools to educate your kids (though you can opt to use them; some people just aren't interested in alternative education). Of course, there are degrees of self-sufficiency; you can aim to have absolutely no contact with utilities or public works, or you can just work toward the ability to do that, in case you need to sometime in the future. For example, I purchase convenience goods from time to time, but I know that if I didn't have that option, I would still be just fine.

2. Off-Grid Basics

When you first consider off-grid living, it sounds like a nearly impossible dream. There are dozens—if not hundreds—of things to think about, and some pretty complicated logistical problems that you'll need to figure out. But one of the things that I believe in very strongly is that by taking things one step at a time, and developing a sound plan, anyone can become totally self-sufficient in a reasonable amount of time. Exactly what "a reasonable amount of time" means is dependent on how much time you're willing to invest. If you're going to quit your job tomorrow and start the process, you could conceivably be totally self-sufficient in a year or two. If you're going to take it more slowly, do a lot of research and some saving, and keep working your current job, you might be looking at more like four or five years before you're completely and totally off the grid. Fortunately, it doesn't look like the world as we know it is going to implode within the next decade or so. But, as I'm fond of saying, you never know.

There are five categories of things that are necessary for successful off-the-grid living: land, housing, electricity, water, and food. I'll go through each of these necessities in the following sections. I strongly recommend reading the entire book before getting started on any of the steps, as there are a lot of things to keep in mind throughout the process. Once you have a better idea of what you're going to need to do on a long-term basis, you can get started.

3. Land

To build a self-sufficient home, you're going to need somewhere to put it. Which means you need land. For many reasons, you'll need rural land, preferably pretty far away from a city—this will ensure that you have enough room to build your home and start planting; keep you out of the reach of utilities, public works, and zoning boards; and potentially provide you with the fuel you need to heat your home and other resources. While completely self-sufficient living in an urban environment is probably possible, it would extremely difficult, and likely very expensive. Also, one of the points of being off the grid is the ability to survive and prosper in case of an economic, political, or technological collapse—and being in a city means you're surrounded by people, all of whom will be vying for resources.

I've broken this section into five different steps, each of which you'll need to undertake in order to get your home up and running. You might not have to complete the steps in this exact order, but this should give you a good idea of where to start and what to do next.

Step 1: Determine How Much land You Need

"How much land do I need?" is always one of the first questions I get asked when discussing going off the grid. I don't have a clear-cut answer; it depends on exactly what you want to do. If you just want enough land for one person in a small cabin, you can get away with about five acres. For most people, though, I don't recommend anything less than 25. This will give you enough space to build a house, plant and cultivate a sizable garden, generate power, and do everything else that you need. Of course, the more land you have, the easier everything is going to be. If you can get 40 acres, I'd recommend it! The amount of land that you buy often depends on how much you're willing to spend; the prices for land can vary widely based on where it is and which natural resources are available on the land. Just to give you an idea of how much you might be looking at, here's a sampling of some land prices (current as of August 2013);

- 40 acres in Gunnison County, Colorado: $88,000—$170,000
- 25 acres in Lane County, Oregon: $239,500
- 37 acres in Navajo County, Arizona: $21,900
- 120 acres in Duchesne County, Utah: $18,000
- 28 acres in Shannon County, Missouri: $38,060

As you can see, where you decide to buy land and what's on that land makes a huge difference. In Utah, where there's a lot of desert and scrubland, you can get a huge parcel of land for very little money. In Oregon, on the other hand, in dense forest, you're looking at a significantly higher cost for less than a quarter of the land. In the middle, you have the property in Missouri, which contains access to some water and forest, for a middling price.

Although setting a budget before starting your search for land might be a good idea, it's often easier to start the search first to get an idea of the range you might be looking at, which depends a lot on where you're willing to live. If you want to live in a high-demand place like Colorado, where there are many ski resorts and outdoorspeople, you'd probably need to be extremely secluded to get a reasonable price. And you also have to consider whether getting through a snowy Colorado winter is something you'd like to try off the grid. It might be very difficult! In contrast, land in places like Arizona and New Mexico is cheaper, because there's less demand—and there, you don't have to worry about the winter (though the summers might be a bit agonizing). The amount of land you need depends heavily on where you want to build your homestead, so do a bit of planning before you start looking for actual pieces of land to save yourself time in the long run.

Finally, when considering different places to build your home, you should take state property laws into account. Because they vary so widely, I recommend speaking to a real estate agent about any possible legal issues you might run up against during this process. If you want to try to get an initial idea of what you might be dealing with, just enter "property law [your state]" in an online search and explore some of the resources that come up.

Step 2: Decide on Whether You're Going to Buy or Build

Many people aren't very interested in building their own home—they'd much rather just buy a house that's ready for self-sufficient living or one that they can easily retrofit. Fortunately, you have quite a few options when it comes to pre-built eco-housing—there are a lot of companies that buy pieces of land and build green homes on them, and sell them to people just like you, who are interested in self-sufficient living. This might be exactly what you're looking for. If you want to buy a home instead of build a new one, this will have a big impact on the land that you end up buying, and it's a good idea to talk to a real estate agent very soon in your land search process, as they likely be able to point you to good resources for your area.

If you're going to be buying a pre-built house, you should go through the considerations in the next chapter before making a decision on the land you purchase. It's a lot easier to put in a bit more legwork early on in the process than retrofit your entire house to fit your self-sufficient lifestyle!

Step 3: Find Land

Before you can buy, build on, and cultivate land, you need to find some! Unfortunately, you can't just drive your 4x4 out into the woods as far as you can go, stick a flag in the ground, and claim your acreage. However, there are quite a few resources that can help you find land that's available. Probably the best way to learn about local land that's available is to speak to a land agent in your area. To find one, just Google "land agent [your state or city]," and you should get a few different results. Explore their website listings, and give them a call. Tell them what you're looking for, and they'll help you get your search underway.

You can also undertake quite a bit of your search online. For the sample prices above, I used LandWatch (www.landwatch.com), a site that provides listings for land available in all 50 states and several other countries. This is a great way to get a general idea of the prices and availability of land in the area you're interested in. If you're not sure whether you can afford land near you, you can use LandWatch to see what you might need to pay for the same amount of land in another state.

Remember that you're going to have to find alternate sources of any natural resources that aren't present on your land. Having some forested land is great, as you can use the trees to heat your home (and cook, if you're really ambitious and want to forego a modern kitchen). A river, stream, or lake is also hugely valuable, as you can provide yourself with water for all of your own needs, including drinking, cooking, and washing. You might even be able to catch some fish! You should also think about access—are there roads that allow you to easily get in and out of the area? Will you need to have roads created? Don't forget that to live somewhere you have to get there first.

Step 4: Buy It!

Once you've picked out a good piece of land, you're ready to pull the trigger! Buy it up before someone else comes along and realizes what a great piece of land it is. You should know ahead of time that it can be difficult to find a bank that will finance undeveloped land, so you might have to pay cash upfront. This means you should start saving soon if this is something you're interested in. Of course, financing isn't impossible to find—you just have to look for the right seller and the right bank.

Step 5: Start Development

You now own land, and you're ready to get started on building your self-sufficient future. It's now time to start on the projects outlined in the next chapters.

4. Housing

One of the first things that you're going to want to do once you've purchased a piece of land is to start getting your housing taken care of. Whether you're going to hire someone to build a house for you, build a cabin yourself, or purchase a pre-fabricated home kit, it's something that will likely take a bit of time, so you should get started early. There are a lot of things you need to think about when it comes to housing, and I'll list a lot of these topics here.

Before I get into the steps you'll need to take to get a house built on your land, I'd like to go over some of the things that are good features to have in a self-sufficient house—this list should be very helpful if you're planning on buying a home instead of building one.

1. Lots of Light

It's really useful to have a lot of natural light coming into your home, both to heat it in the winter and to use less electricity for lighting. Plus it's just nice to have a well-lit home.

2. Solar Panels

Providing electricity for your home is an important consideration, so if you're able to buy a house with solar panels already on it, that's great. If not, make sure that your roof will receive a lot of light throughout the day so you can maximize your solar collection (true-south-facing roofs are best). If you're buying a house, finding one with solar panels already installed on the roof is a huge bonus, as having a set installed can cost a lot of money—up to and over $10,000, depending on how much energy you need and whether you have other sources of power available.

3. Insulation

Heating and cooling a house uses a lot of energy, so having a well-insulated home is a must. You'll keep heat inside in the winter and allow it to escape in the summer. Choosing environmentally friendly insulation options is always recommended, but you might not have this option if you're buying a home that's already been built, unless you're willing to have it re-insulated.

Double-paned and well-insulated windows are also very beneficial. So, even if you decide not to re-insulate your entire home, you may still want to consider swapping out the windows.

4. Eco-Friendly Appliances

Whether or not you have a washing machine, dishwasher, refrigerator, or TV is up to you, but if you want them, it's a good idea to make sure that they're as environmentally friendly as possible. This means that they're efficient, and don't waste energy. This also applies to things like shower heads, toilets, and other plumbing fixtures.

The characteristics of a green home vary widely, and you might find that your particular environment requires different structural features. However, the above four will go a long way in preparing your house to be self-sufficient. So if you're going to be purchasing a home, these should be high on your list of important inclusions.

With that said, here are some important steps for building your own house on a plot of land you've purchased.

1. Claiming your land

As soon as you buy a piece of land, you should put some sort of shelter on it so that other people know that it's yours. It doesn't need to be much—a small trailer or pop-up camper would be fine. Even a large lean-to would do. Not only is it a good idea to stake your claim, but if you're going to be building your own home, you'll want to keep your tools and materials out of the elements, so something like a carport cover would work perfectly.

2. Type of Housing

This is likely going to be the biggest decision you'll make in regards to your housing. A lot of this comes down to how much work you want to put into creating a living space for yourself. Some people believe that an important part of self-sufficient living is to rely on as few traditional companies and organizations as possible, which means they generally prefer to build their own homes. I find this pretty admirable, but building things isn't really one of my strengths, so I chose to hire a builder. This is totally fine. You can also land somewhere in the middle of these two options by using a modular, pre-fabricated option. Whichever route you choose to go, one thing to always keep in mind when considering your housing needs is that your home should be as eco-friendly and efficient as possible. This might impact the type of house that you want to build—for example, rammed earth houses and cob houses are made of organic materials, and are very well insulated, meaning you'll use less energy to modulate the temperature.

A small self-sufficient home.

Of course, there are price differences here, too. Some modular homes can be built for around $150,000, while larger, custom homes can run you upwards of several hundred thousand dollars. Building your new home is going to be the most expensive part of the entire off-the-grid process, unless you bought a parcel of extremely prime land (buying expensive land and building a more affordable house actually isn't a bad idea; that usually means you'll have a lot of natural resources on your property and a small house that doesn't require a lot of upkeep).

3. Who's going to build?

No matter what kind of house you decide on, you're going to have to decide whether you're going to build it yourself or have someone else build it. Obviously, having someone else do the building is going to require less effort on your part, though it will likely be more expensive. This might be a convenience that you're willing to pay for, though, because building a house on your own, even with quite a bit of help, is a lot of work!

Construction of a rammed earth house.

If you've decided to hire a builder, you'll have to find one that can build a house to the specifications that you require (see the next section of this chapter for more details on things you'll want to include in your house). Not all builders are able or willing to do this, so you might have to find a good eco-friendly builder in your area. It's best to ask a real estate agent who to get in touch with, as not all builders have websites, and the eco-friendly niche is a small one. Before you have your house plans drawn up, it's a good idea to get in touch with several builders to discuss your requirements and the logistical difficulties of building a house in a remote area—hopefully after talking to a few builders, one or two of them will have risen to the top of the list as obvious choices.

If you're going to do the building yourself, I recommend getting a good idea of who's going to help you early in the process. If you want to get the house done quickly, you're going to need a lot of help, so you should call up your friends and family and see who'd be willing to give you a hand. (I recommend offering pizza and beer as a reward to willing workers!)

4. Drafting plans

No matter who's going to build your house, you'll need a plan. If you're hiring a builder, you can work with them to draw up a set of plans for a completely customized house that fits all of your needs, which is really convenient. The more of the features you have at the beginning, the fewer you're going to have to retrofit later. Of course, having plans drawn up for you adds time and expense to the process, which is something you may not want (as I stressed in the introduction, however, taking this process slowly and being very patient is highly recommended). But it will likely save you time and money in the long run.

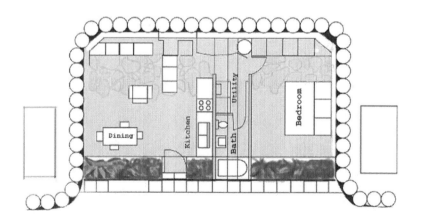

ONE BEDROOM

Plans for a one-bedroom Earthship sustainable home.

The other option, which is available no matter who's building your home, is to use plans that have already been drawn up. Some companies have already gone through the planning and designing process for a number of off-the-grid homes and have put them up for sale online, where you can purchase the plans and give them to your builder (or start building yourself). www.offgridshelters.com and www.earthship.com are two sites that you can check out to get an idea of what you might be able to purchase. Keep in mind that plans aren't cheap—while some of the ones available are just $250, you can pay up to $8,000 for a three-bedroom Earthship plan.

5. Start building!

Once you have your land and you've decided on a builder, you're ready to start building! If you did your research, you shouldn't have any problems with land or water laws, zoning regulations, or any other legal issues. If you hired a builder, you can sit back and watch your house go up. If, on the other hand, you decided to build yourself, it's time to start buying materials and hauling them up to the site of your new home (the carport cover or lean-to you put up earlier will help keep everything protected from the weather). As I mentioned before, I'm not a builder myself, so that's really all I know about building a house. Consult the resources that I listed above to learn more about building your own eco-friendly home to get a better idea of what, exactly, you'll need to do at this stage.

5. Electricity

Now that you have your house sorted, it's time to get your power supply up and running. Having access to electricity—while not strictly a necessity—is something that nearly everyone is going to want, especially if you have a family. Living off the grid does entail giving up some things, but you don't have to give up power! I mentioned earlier in the book that you won't have to give up modern luxuries to live self-sufficiently, and the fact that you can provide your own power is one of the main reasons that this is the case. Easy access to unlimited electricity at all times is one of the biggest advantages of living on the grid, so it's easy to see why people are hesitant to give self-sufficient living a try. But with a good setup, you can provide yourself with enough power to run your appliances and some luxury items as well. Of course, the more power you need, the more power-supplying technology you're going to have to invest in, but green energy can end up saving you a lot of money in the long run.

I'll discuss green energy sources first, and then move onto more traditional methods of power production. It will usually be necessary to use a combination of methods to make sure that you can provide enough power for your household, especially in environments where one type of energy source may not always be available (think of trying to power your use using a solar generator in Washington or Oregon—it's not always going to be very reliable).

Solar Power

There are two different types of solar power: generators and paneling. Solar generators store energy that have been collected by solar panels in a battery so that it can be used whenever it's needed. Many solar generators come with small sets of panels attached. How much energy the generator can provide depends on the size of the generator—some will charge your phone, while others will run your refrigerator for most of a day on a single charge. Many people like solar generators for varied applications because they're silent and they produce no emissions, which make them much more attractive than fossil-fuel-powered generators.

A portable solar generator and panels.

You've probably seen solar panels on the roofs of some houses in your city. While they're not exactly common, they're becoming more widespread as an alternative energy source. Unfortunately, having solar panels installed on the roof of your house can be quite expensive (up to and exceeding $10,000 in some cases). However, because they're elevated, they'll get a lot of sun, making them one of the best investments you can make in green energy for your self-sufficient home. While you might be able to get away without them on a cabin or a very small house, I would recommend having them installed on anything more significant, as you're likely to need quite a bit of power. If you're careful with your electricity usage, you can power your entire house from these panels, but it's always good to have redundant backup systems.

Wind Power

Wind farms—collections of dozens or hundreds of electricity-generating wind turbines—are popping up all over the place, and they're proving to be a viable source of clean energy. You can harness the power of the wind on your own property, and if you understand the principles behind correctly placing and operating turbines, you can actually generate quite a bit of power with them! Of course, these are best used in a windy part of the country, because if the wind dies down, you'll be running on stored power, which is limited. No matter where you live, the wind won't be constant, so it's important to combine these with a backup generator of some sort.

A small, residential wind generator.

Hiring a contractor to install these on your land is a must, as they're complicated pieces of mechanical and electrical machinery, and they're quite sensitive (which is why they often need adjustments and repairs, something you should keep in mind when considering wind power), which means an experienced professional should be consulted when it comes to placing, building, and maintaining them.

Hydro Power

Using water to generate electricity can be a great way to power your home if you live near a stream or river. Major hydroelectric power generators are often run in dams in rivers and lakes, and can generate quite a bit of power. Smaller-scale equipment is available that can also generate enough electricity to power a small home. If you're able to use multiple hydroelectric generators, you could conceivably power a larger home. One of the big advantages of using hydro power is that it's almost always constant—it's quite rare that a stream or river will completely dry up, even if it goes down a bit during drier seasons. If there's a drought, however, you might find that you have trouble generating enough power for your home. Similarly, flooding can damage or destroy your equipment, so relying totally on hydro power is advisable only if you live in an area that's not susceptible to either of these circumstances.

Gasoline Generators

Whether or not you want to keep a gas-power generator on hand depends a lot on how you feel about a connection to civilization—while a generator will allow you to supply your own power, you'll also need to go into town occasionally to buy gas, which many people see as defeating the purpose of self-sufficient living. It also introduces noxious fumes into the atmosphere, making it a very environmentally unfriendly energy source, which is another thing that many people see as antithetical to the principles behind living off the grid. However, keeping a gas generator on hand can be useful in case your renewable energy sources are unavailable for a short period of time.

Gasoline does have some advantages as a fuel: it burns at a relatively low temperature, making the generator itself less of a fire hazard than something like propane, which burns hotter. Gasoline is also something that's widely available, so it's not hard to fill up your stores (for now, at least—there's no telling how long that will be the case). However, gas generators need to be kept outside because of the fumes they produce, which means you'll have to go outside—rain or shine, pleasant or freezing—to get it started up. And they're loud, too, which a lot of people don't like. And if you're preparing yourself for a catastrophe, you may want to keep in mind that running a gas generator sends a signal for miles around that you have resources, which could attract unwanted visitors.

When you first get up to your plot of land, you might want to keep a small gas generator on hand to power tools and similar things, especially if you're going to be building your own home. And it never hurts to have a little extra backup. But you won't find too many green self-sufficient homes that rely on a gas generator for more than occasional backup power.

Ethanol Generators

Using ethanol, which can be derived from corn, is much more environmentally friendly than using a gasoline generator, and storing corn oil is a lot safer than keeping a stockpile of gasoline in or near your house. One thing that you need to keep in mind if you're interested in using ethanol to power your home is how you're going to get corn oil—you can either buy and store it or make it yourself. Of course, buying it is much easier, but it still keeps you tied to civilization. Making your own corn oil, however, is a very involved and time-consuming process and requires a lot of corn. The best resource that I've found for home corn oil extraction is at http://www.ehow.com/how_4924078_extract-oil-corn.html. An ethanol generator is a great way to provide backup power to your home if your primary renewable energy source is temporarily unavailable, and I encourage you to consider investing in one. Whether you make or store corn oil is up to you, but you can be sure that your homestead will be much more environmentally friendly than if you use gasoline.

Providing your own power to your house requires some relatively complex electrical circuitry, and I definitely recommend getting an experienced electrician to get you set up to do this. Having this system incorrectly installed could be very dangerous, especially if your house is still hooked up to the power grid. There are plenty of books available on how to power your house with renewable energy that will teach you how to do this, or you can just hire an electrician to make sure you get set up correctly. No matter what you decide to do, don't just turn the generator on and try to figure it out!

6. Water

Something that many people don't realize is that you need *a lot* of water to keep your house up and running. You use water for all sorts of things—drinking, cooking, washing, cleaning, and running many of your appliances all require water, and you're going to need to supply it somehow. Like power, water is one of the things that most people rely on public services for, but you'll definitely need to supply it for yourself if you're going to be totally self-sufficient. Fortunately, water is an abundant natural resource, and there are quite a few ways in which you can collect it and prepare it for use. It can be a little expensive to get your system set up at first, but once you've established an effective method for providing water for your home, it will, for the most part, continue running on its own with few problems.

I'll start with ways of collecting water, and then discuss ways of purifying and preparing it for use, as well as dealing with waste.

Rain Water

If you live somewhere with a decent amount of rainfall, collecting rain water can actually be an effective way of meeting most of your needs (this is great in the Pacific Northwest, where it rains all the time; it might not work very well in places like Utah, Arizona, or Texas). You can use a few different methods to collect rain water—one of the simplest ways is to simply place a large number of small containers around your property. Milk jugs with the tops cut off work well for this, as do buckets. You can hang dozens of them in trees or place them on your patio and, if you get enough rain, they'll actually supply a surprising amount of water for your home. Of course, the more of these containers you have, the more rain water you'll be able to collect. You can also use a single large container, called a cistern, which can be made of concrete, metal, plastic, or fiberglass. This is usually a large container (some of them are a good 8 feet tall) that sits above ground to collect rain water.It can also be attached to a piping system that's drilled down to groundwater level to supplement the water you collect from the rain.

A rain cistern that collects runoff water.

One thing that you should keep in mind when you're considering collecting rain water is that any environmental pollutants that are common in your area are likely to be in the rain water you collect. So if you live somewhere with a lot of air pollution, this might not be the safest method of providing water for your home. Of course, you'll purify any water that you're going to consume, but it's still a good idea to use as clean a source of water as possible for all of the activities that you'll need water for. You can get information on air pollution levels in your area at www.airnow.gov.

Well Drilling

Probably the most common way of supplying water to your property is through the drilling of a well, because groundwater is everywhere. No matter where you are, it's likely that you'll be able to drill down to the level of groundwater and use it to supply your needs. It's best to hire a drilling specialist, who will come and check out your land to determine the best placement and depth of the well. They'll also be able to drill in a way that reduces water waste and contamination. This isn't likely to be cheap (well-drilling is usually priced by the foot, and you can expect to pay around $5,000), but if you can get someone to dig a deep well, you'll have a consistent source of clean water for a very long time, regardless of whether or not you get rain. One of the biggest advantages of drilling is that you can decide with ease exactly how your water supply is used—you can send water to your kitchen and laundry room, to your garden irrigation, or to your bathroom for a hot shower.

Springs

If you're really lucky (or you do a great job of purchasing land) you might actually be able to use a natural spring as your source of water! There are some risks involved in this, as it's always possible that the groundwater feeding the spring is contaminated, but if you're careful and you test and purify your water really well, you can actually get quite a lot of water from a spring. There's really no more self-sufficient method of getting water than that.

Buying Water

Of course, you can always buy your water supply (or at least part of it) from someone else. Obviously, this goes against the ideals of many people's vision of off-the-grid living, but if you're just getting started, or you need a lot of extra water for a day—like if you're having visitors—it's something you can consider. The best way to get a price estimate is to search online for "water hauling [your state]" and call a few providers; the price often depends on how much water you want and where you live. You'll need somewhere for this water to go—usually it's a cistern or a well. If there's a societal meltdown, this option isn't going to be available, so if this is something you're worried about, it's recommendable to not rely on this strategy. And even if you do decide to buy a portion of your water supply, you should have a backup source, just in case you need it (the rain traps discussed above are low-maintenance, easy to use, and pretty unobtrusive).

Purifying Your Water

If you don't properly purify your water, you may be exposing yourself to harmful chemicals or bacteria The two most common methods of purifying water are boiling and iodine. To disinfect water by boiling, bring it to a roiling boil and keep it there for at least one minute (if you're at high altitude, aim for at least four minutes). After you've let it cool, store it in a clean container (discussed below). This will kill off a lot of the illness-causing bacteria and microorganisms present in the water. It's best to combine it with a chemical solution for disinfecting to make sure you clean it out as much as possible. To use iodine, add five drops (ten drops if the water is cloudy) of 2% iodine solution (this is the strength you'll find in first-aid-grade iodine) to each quart of water (a quart is about the same size as a liter). Let it sit for 30 minutes before using.

Another method that's fairly common is to use commercially prepared disinfecting tablets, which usually contain chlorine or iodine. Just follow the instructions on the packaging—usually you'll just need to drop a tablet in a quart or liter of water. Although it sounds like a bad idea, using bleach to purify your water is actually extremely effective; just add 1/8 teaspoon of unscented, liquid household bleach to a gallon of water, stir it, and let it sit for 30 minutes. If the water doesn't have a slight chlorine smell after 30 minutes, add the same amount of bleach again and let it sit for 15 minutes.[1] Many people also use a more natural, sunlight-based method that consists of placing the water in clear plastic PET bottles and letting them sit in direct sunlight for six hours. Although I can't recommend this, it's definitely better than not purifying your water at all!

----

[1]These instructions assume that you're using a standard household bleach that consists of 4–6% bleach. If your bleach is around 1% chlorine, you'll need more like 5/8 teaspoon. And if you have particularly strong bleach, in the 7–10% range, you'll only need 1/16 teaspoon.

As I mentioned before, you might be surprised at how much water you need to use to keep your home running, especially if you have a family. If you want to get an estimate of what you might use in a day, I recommend going to http://ga.water.usgs.gov/edu/sq3.html—by answering a few questions, you'll receive an estimate of how much water your household uses in 24 hours. Of course, it could be quite accurate or very inaccurate, depending on the appliances in your home and how accurately you answer the questions. If you want a more accurate estimate, you can go to http://www.wecalc.org/calc; you'll need to answer a lot more questions, but you'll get a better idea of what you're using. To give you a really rough idea, a friend of mine used the first site to estimate his water usage—he lives in a small apartment, and uses an estimated 53 gallons per day. That's a lot of water for one person!

Two uses of water that you might not have thought of in the past are irrigation and sewage. If you're going to be self-sufficient, you'll need to provide your own food, and that requires quite a lot of water, especially if you live in an arid climate. You'll need to water your plants, which can be a significant amount of water (I recommend *Western Garden Book of Edibles* as a great reference on how much you'll need to water your plants, and anything else you could possibly want to know about gardening). And if you're going to be raising animals on your property, you'll need to provide them with enough water, too. Remember to take this into account when you're tallying your projected water needs.

Most people don't remember a time when we had to think at all about our waste and what to do with it; with public sewer systems and modern plumbing, you just use the toilet and flush it—no more thought or effort required. However, if you're going to completely cut yourself off from utility companies, you're going to have to get used to the idea of dealing with your own waste. The simplest way is to use an outhouse, which is nothing more than a small shed with a toilet in it—the toilet is placed over a deep hole in the ground, which will hold all of your waste and allow it to be reabsorbed into the earth. It may seem strange now, but people have been doing this for thousands of years! Modern plumbing is really a very recent technological advance. It's a good idea to move your outhouse once or twice a year so that it can be placed over a new hole and the old one can be covered up. Also, make sure to place your outhouse downhill (or very far away from) your well—you don't want to contaminate your water supply.

The other option that you have is to get a septic system installed—this consists of a septic tank, which is buried deep underground, that collects, stores, and treats your waste, releasing treated wastewater back into the ground. It can be expensive to get one of these installed (most are in the $4,000–$5,000 range), but if you want the convenience of modern plumbing, it's really your only option.

7. Food

After figuring out your water needs and supply, you should start thinking about what you're going to eat once you move off the grid. It can be daunting, trying to plan your diet and figuring out how to provide all (or at least most) of your own food, but if you take the time to plan and consider your options, you should have no problem coming up with a viable food provision method.

Vegetarian or Carnivorous Living

To simplify things, the first issue you need to decide on is if you're going to eat meat. It might seem like being a vegetarian would make everything easier, as you wouldn't have to raise animals, but remember that you have to get the protein you need to survive, so not eating meat actually makes things a bit more complicated in some respects. You can certainly maintain a healthy diet whether you eat meat or not—whether you decide to live a vegetarian (or vegan) lifestyle is up to you.

It's also possible that you could live a primarily vegetarian lifestyle and produce enough food on your land to support this lifestyle, but continue to occasionally buy meat from a store. That way, you can enjoy eating meat without the extra effort of raising animals, but you could also be confident that you'd be able to continue living self-sufficiently if something bad happens and you're no longer able to buy meat.

Gardening

No matter what you've decided on the previous point, you're going to need a garden. Growing your own vegetables is by far the easiest and most efficient way of providing yourself with the calories you need, and it can be done successfully almost anywhere, as long as you take your area's climate into account when planning your garden. For example, in the Midwest, you might want to plant a bit later in the year than you would further south, in case of a late cold snap. Because every area is different, I highly recommend going to a gardening store to buy your first seeds and asking the employees there for tips on how to best plant and harvest your garden. You'll get a lot of great information this way, and it'll save you a lot of time in online searching.

So what might you want to plant? The best things to start with are hearty vegetables—things like potatoes, green beans, broccoli, cauliflower, cucumbers, corn, carrots, soy, and squash. These are the kinds of vegetables that you can easily build a full diet around (though if, like me, you're a bit wary of the hormone-like substances in soy, you might want to skip it). Of course, you can plant whatever you want—tomatoes, rhubarb, artichokes, cabbage, onions, peppers, peas, asparagus, spinach, Brussels sprouts . . . the sky is the limit. Just remember that you need to grow the things that will help provide the necessary calories for you and your family throughout the entire year. No one's going to be very happy if you're stuck with a meal of rhubarb and onions at the end of the winter. Planting vegetables in the right season will help you a lot in this area—again, I recommend consulting the *Western Garden Book of Edibles*. You can also check out a nifty tool at http://eatseasonably.co.uk/what-to-eat-now/calendar/ that will help you determine when you should be planting certain vegetables.

Again, seeking local knowledge is the best thing you can do here—if some vegetables don't grow well in your area, someone at a gardening store will know. Take advantage of the information you can find right in your hometown; you might be surprised at how much you can learn by just asking.

While you can easily plant a garden in the soil that's already around your house, you have a few options that will help make your garden more successful. For example, you can create raised beds to better manage the soil and fertilizer that go into your garden, and make it easier to keep track of rotating your crops, which is crucial for long-term success. There are a lot of different ways to build raised beds, but I prefer the simpler methods, one of which is detailed here: http://www.anythingpretty.com/2009/03/how-to-vegetable-garden-beds-part-1.html. If you're looking for an assortment of different plans that cover a variety of complexity levels, check out this page: http://tipnut.com/raised-garden-beds/.

Another option for improving the yield of your garden is to create hoop houses, which are very simple greenhouses—these protect your plants and give you a longer growing season, which is especially valuable if your homestead is in a cold climate. I strongly recommend using a hoop house, especially if there's going to be more than one person depending on your vegetables. For more information on hoop houses, visit www.hoopbenders.net. This site also sells the materials you need for hoop houses at affordable prices.

A small hoop house.

Finally, I'll note that starting your vegetable garden before you actually move onto your homestead is a good idea. You don't want to have small plants that are susceptible to small fluctuations in the weather when you move in—you want to have fully grown, yielding plants. You have two options here: if you currently live decently close to your future homestead, you can plant the garden there and go out and tend to it occasionally. If not, you can plant them in large pots and haul them up to your homestead when you move. You also might be able to buy full-sized plants from a nursery before you move. It's also possible to buy and bring enough food to get you through the first few months of the growing season, but then you would have to worry about storage and possible spoilage, so I wouldn't recommend risking it.

Orchards

I know that the word "orchard" is probably very intimidating to most people, but growing trees is just like growing any other plant—they're just a bit bigger! It takes more time for trees to grow enough to start bearing fruit (or nuts, depending on what kind of trees you plant), so you should either start these very early or transplant some trees that have been started and are almost ready to bear. Trees have several benefits other than providing food, including preventing erosion on your land, and providing shade, which will help protect your other plants from overexposure to the sun and give you some great shady spots in your yard.

Again, the types of trees that you can grow on your land depend on where you live. Apple trees can survive almost anywhere, and peach trees are also pretty versatile. If you live in the right climate, almond, walnut, plum, orange, apricot, pear, cherry, and avocado trees can also be grown successfully.

Raising Animals

If you've decided that you can't (or just don't want to) give up meat, you're going to have raise your own animals. In the United States, we're tragically disconnected from the source of our meat, and this makes many people uncomfortable with the idea of raising and slaughtering animals for meat. But this is something that you're going to have to get over if you want to provide your family with meat!

Pigs, sheep, and rabbits are all commonly raised for meat, and both chickens and turkeys are relatively easy to care for as well. Choosing which of these animals you're going to raise on your property depends both on what you're looking for and how much work you're willing to put in. If you just want meat, and you don't need a lot of it, rabbits are definitely the way to go. A hutch, some equipment (like watering bottles and food dishes), some food, and a few rabbits will probably cost you less than $250, which isn't bad at all. And rabbits are known for their breeding capabilities, so you shouldn't have any problem replacing the stock that you put on the table! If you're looking for a more multi-purpose animal, Icelandic sheep and laying hens are both good choices. You can get wool, milk, and meat from the sheep, and hens will give you eggs and meat. For more information on raising hens, check out my other book "Beginner's Backyard Chickens." You can find it on Amazon's Store.

Hunting, Fishing, and Gathering

One nice thing about living closer to nature is that nature can actually provide you with quite a bit of food. Unless you're living in the desert, there's likely plenty of food available for you if you're willing to work for it. Your first option is hunting—and if you're thinking about living off the grid, there's a decent chance that you've done some 60 or more pounds of meat, which will keep you fed for quite a while. If you live in places where there's wild boar, you can expect around the same amount of meat. (As an aside, I have a friend who hunts boar and makes his own sausage; it's amazing.) If you decide that you're interested in hunting, you should first look into the local laws; you'll likely need a license for your gun or bow, and a hunting license as well, which allows you to take a certain number of animals per year. Using a gun or bow is up to you—a gun is easier, but many people like to use a bow because of the feeling of accomplishment that it gives them or because they feel a little closer to nature.

What you hunt depends largely on where you are—deer can be found pretty much anywhere, and wild birds like turkey, duck, and pheasant are also quite common. Wild boar and elk are less prevalent, but can definitely be found in certain parts of the country. Rabbits and squirrels, though they're pretty small, are absolutely everywhere, and are great practice if you're teaching your kids to hunt. Of course, it's good to remember that if you're going to hunt animals for food, you're going to have to learn to dress and, most likely, butcher them yourself. If you're interested in this, I recommend *The Complete Book of Butchering, Smoking, Curing, and Sausage Making* by Philip Hasheider.

Fishing is another common way to provide some food for your homestead. If you live near a river or a lake (or the ocean, though available land near the ocean is pretty rare) you can likely find some common game fish that you can catch. Large- and smallmouth bass, walleye, trout, catfish, crappie, muskelunge, and sunfish are all common around the country. If you'd like to learn to identify the fish in your area and determine how to catch them, check out *Basic Fishing: A Beginner's Guide* by Wade Bourne. Like with land animals, you'll need to prepare the fish for eating yourself.

While gathering isn't something that a lot of people think to do, it can actually be a good way to supplement your diet. Again, depending on where you live, you'll have different options. My wife loves to pick blackberries when they're in season and turn them into jams and pies. If you're living in a temperate climate, there are almost certainly berries and nuts that you can pick off of bushes or the ground. I recommend reading the information at http://www.motherearthnews.com/organic-gardening/edible-wild-plants.aspx first, though, to make sure that you're not going to eat something that'll make you sick.

What to Do with Extra Food

It's important to remember that food is going to be most plentiful in the warm seasons than it is in winter, so it's a good idea to collect more than you need and save some of it. I've written an entire book on preserving and storing food, but I can give you a couple quick options here (I recommend doing more research to see which preservation methods you're interested in.)

Canning is a really common way to preserve food, and has the advantage that you can do it with just about anything. You don't need much equipment—just a big pot and some canning jars is enough to get you started. Properly canned food will last a really long time, especially in a cooler environment, like a basement or a dark cupboard. As long as the seal stays intact, you should have no problem with your food going bad. Most people think of jams, jellies, fruits, and vegetables when they think of canned foods, but you can easily can meat and dairy products as well.

Freezing is also very common, and, like canning, works with almost everything. Meat, dairy, and fruits all freeze well, and most vegetables (with the exception of leafy ones like spinach and cabbage) freeze and thaw quite well. The big disadvantage of freezing is that it requires a constant flow of energy, which means you'll need to provide a lot of electricity for your freezer. If you don't have a problem with this, though, it's an easy way to preserve your food. All you have to do is put it in a freezer bag and toss it in the freezer! Of course, if your power goes out, you might be scrambling to find other preservation methods very quickly.

Smoking, drying, and salting are generally used for meats, but fruits and vegetables can also be dried to increase their shelf life. If you've done a good job with the process, food can last a long time at room temperature, though it's safer to keep it refrigerated, frozen, or canned (using multiple preservation methods will help keep your food safe for you to eat for a much longer period of time).

The important thing is that you find some way or another to keep your food from spoiling over the winter, when you'll be less able to procure it (unless you're going to be buying a lot of your food, of course). Try different methods and see what you like, or talk to someone who's experienced in food preservation and ask them for suggestions.

8. Emergency Preparedness

While a lot of people view self-sufficient living as a way to be prepared for catastrophes, you still need to be ready for smaller-scale issues. You never know when illness might strike you or one of your family members, and the risk of things like fires, floods, and other environmental events is ever-present. Living off the grid often means working with tools, too, increasing the chance that you might hurt yourself. And, if you're like me, there's always a good chance that you'll kick something by accident or cut yourself with a knife while chopping vegetables and need to bandage yourself up.

Being ready in case of an emergency has been the topic of numerous books, seminars, and websites, so I'll only go into basics here. I strongly recommend reading a more thorough resource to familiarize yourself with the more in-depth principles that I don't have the room to discuss here, but this will give you a good start.

1. Get First-Aid and CPR Certified

I can't stress the importance of this enough—not only if you're going off the grid, but just for everyday life. First aid covers things like checking someone for injuries, cleaning and bandaging small wounds, creating small splints, and things like that. While cardiopulmonary resuscitation (CPR) is extremely effective in medical dramas, it's not quite the same miracle lifesaver in real life, but it does increase someone's chances of surviving a heart attack. While it's fairly unlikely that you'll ever need to know anything like that, it's much better to be prepared, especially when a first aid training can be as short as a single day. If you feel that you'd like to get a more comprehensive training, getting certified as a first responder is a good idea—you'll learn things like triage, automatic external defibrillator (AED) use, broken bone immobilization, and patient transport.

2. Keep a First-Aid Kit

This might seem like an obvious one, but you should always have a first-aid kit on hand. And not one of those tiny ones that has ten adhesive bandages and some anti-bacterial ointment. The kit should have many different sizes of bandages, gauze, anti-bacterial ointment, a pair of scissors, tweezers, a nail clipper, rubber gloves, and some safety pins. Many companies make first-aid kits that pack a lot of tools into a small case, and you can always create one of your own with a small duffel bag or backpack. The Red Cross recommends the following for a family of four:

- 2 absorbent compress dressings (5 x 9 inches)
- 25 adhesive bandages (assorted sizes)
- 1 adhesive cloth tape (10 yards x 1 inch)
- 5 antibiotic ointment packets (approximately 1 gram)
- 5 antiseptic wipe packets
- 2 packets of aspirin (81 mg each)
- 1 blanket (space blanket)
- 1 breathing barrier (with one-way valve)
- 1 instant cold compress
- 2 pair of non-latex gloves (size: large)
- 2 hydrocortisone ointment packets (approximately 1 gram each)
- Scissors
- 1 roller bandage (3 inches wide)
- 1 roller bandage (4 inches wide)
- 5 sterile gauze pads (3 x 3 inches)
- 5 sterile gauze pads (4 x 4 inches)
- Oral thermometer (non-mercury/nonglass)
- 2 triangular bandages
- Tweezers
- First aid instruction booklet

I also recommend keeping a flashlight in your first-aid kit, in case you have to help someone out in the dark. You should have at least one kit at home and one in your car.

3. Develop an Emergency Plan

Every household should have an emergency plan in case of a disaster. Like I said before, you never know what might be coming. Creating an effective plan requires that everyone in your house is on the same page, and it takes some time and effort to put together. This keeps a lot of people from doing it. That being said, it's extremely important to be prepared, especially if you're going to be living in an isolated location. The best resource that I can recommend for creating a family emergency plan is at http://emergency.cdc.gov/preparedness/plan/. It covers the process in more detail than I could in this book. And for all things related to emergency preparedness, visit http://emergency.cdc.gov/planning/. The personal section is probably the most useful for homesteaders, but there's information on specific types of emergencies as well, which you might find interesting.

4. Keep Your Vehicles Prepared

If you live in a city, this isn't as big of a deal, but living in the wilderness (or at least closer to it) makes it much more important, especially if you live in a place that tends to get a lot of snow. In the summer, keeping your vehicle prepared amounts to keeping a first-aid kit in the trunk and making sure that your gas tank never gets below half (or, even better, 3/4) full. In the winter, however, you should have a winter-specific car emergency kit that includes warm clothing, grit, reflectors, and tire chains, along with your regular first-aid kit.

A homemade winter car emergency kit.

Photo credit: Cindy Compton

And if you live in the mountains or in a very cold climate, having an engine block heater isn't a bad idea, either, so you can get your car started a little more quickly. These are things you'll need to think about.

5. Make Sure You Can Continue Communication

One of the most valuable things in an emergency situation is effective communication. There's always the possibility that you'll get separated from your family or anyone else in your group, and being able to maintain communication will make finding each other and coordinating your activities much easier. Just about everyone has a cell phone, and this helps quite a bit, but you can't always count on cell networks being operational in an emergency, so it's a good idea to have a backup set of small walkie-talkies or something similar that each member of your family can grab at a moment's notice. Your emergency plan should address the need for communication and make recommendations on how to get in contact with one another and specify a designated meeting place.

6. Always Have Food Stockpiled

In the previous chapter, I mentioned that you should be collecting extra food when you're able so that you have enough to get you and your family through the winter. It's also important to have enough food to keep you going during an emergency situation. With proper canning, it's easy to have at least a month's worth of food stored in your basement or garage. Your emergency supply of food should only be used in case of emergency—if you just want that extra can of peaches that's in the stash, you'll have to be disciplined and leave it there, or else you'll find your supply dwindling, which is something that you definitely don't want to discover if there's a natural disaster or some other sort of emergency. A month's worth of food is a good place to start, but having two or even three month's worth is better (if you have room for it, of course).

As I mentioned, these are just the basics of emergency preparedness; if you want to get a more comprehensive idea of how to prepare your family and your home for an emergency, visit http://emergency.cdc.gov/planning/ or read *Handbook to Practical Disaster Preparedness for the Family* by Dr. Arthur Bradley.

9. Off-The-Grid Family and Social life

Living a self-sufficient life by yourself is one thing; doing it with a family is entirely another. Going off the grid with your family can certainly be done, but it adds another level of complexity—both practical and emotional—to your transition. Your family (nuclear and extended) and friends might think you're crazy for wanting to go off the grid, and you'll have to explain over, and over again what you're doing. You'll have to tell people all about the advantages of self-sufficiency, explain how you're going to deal with the difficulties, and generally defend your decision repeatedly. This isn't much fun, but eventually everyone calms down and gets used to your new style of living.

Besides that, there are some things that you will have to plan for. I've listed three important ones here that will help you start thinking about the kinds of things you'll have to consider.

1. Staying Connected

When you're on the grid, you constantly have access to your cell phone and the internet, no matter where you are. Which means that e-mail, Facebook, Twitter, and about fifteen other kinds of instant communication are always available. If you want to get in touch with someone, all you have to do is tap out a quick text message. That's not the case when you're living off the grid. If you choose to have a cell phone, you might not get very consistent reception, and mobile data is likely to be quite slow. Having an internet connection at your house can also be difficult, as moving away from cities generally gets you out of range of the fiber-optic cables that carry bandwidth.

However, there are several satellite internet providers that you can contract with to provide you with internet, helping you stay connected. Satellite phones are also available, though they tend to be quite expensive. You can certainly live without these things, but I don't recommend it. Staying in touch with your friends and family is really important, not only

54

for your social wellbeing, but also for your mental health. Being completely isolated is hard, and not very many people enjoy it, especially for an extended period of time! Make sure to find a way to keep in touch with your community. If you have kids, this is next to essential: they're not likely to be very excited about moving far away from their friends, but being able to stay in touch will help.

Equally as important is getting in touch with a new community—even if you go really far out into the wilderness, if there's a road to drive on, it will almost certainly take you to a town, village, or country truck stop within a couple of hours. You'll probably have to go there to pick up supplies every once in a while, and you might even find that you go occasionally just for a change of scenery. Talk to people while you're there! Get to know business owners and other locals (even if there are only a couple and they live a good 10 miles away from you). People who live far out in the country are usually a pretty accepting lot, as they have similar interests. They might not be too happy if you're living right next door to them, but as long as you're not invading their space, you should find it easy to be friendly with them.

2. Educating Your Kids

This can be a tough issue—most states have laws requiring children to complete a certain amount of education, and if you're not providing it, you can get in big trouble. But it's going to be very difficult for your kids to attend a traditional public school, as you're likely to be far away from any place that would provide one. Fortunately, there are several options. Check www.k12.com to see if your state has an online schooling program—you might be surprised to find out that many do. www.abcmouse.com and www.starfall.com both provide resources on online schooling that you might find useful. Keep in mind that online schooling may require some face-to-face interaction that you will have to administer or provide transportation to.

Because there are a lot of people that live a good distance from civilization, there are often educational programs available for kids. Rural charter schools can be found in many areas, and they're often well-adapted for off-the-grid living. Some of them only require classroom work a few days a week, so the time you spend driving your child to and from school will be limited. The biggest advantage of this method of schooling is that your kids still have social interactions with other children, which is very important in their social and mental development.

And, of course, there's homeschooling. Taking your child's education totally into your own hands is always an option, and it may be the best one, depending on where you live. Homeschooling isn't nearly as challenging or intimidating as it sounds—there are many different programs that have been vetted and published by professional educators that you can use, ensuring that your child will receive a proper education. Like the online schooling option, however, your child will receive little interaction with other kids, which isn't good.

It's important to make sure that your child gets to make friends, even if you live way out in a rural area. As I mentioned before, there are often small collections of people (like extended neighborhoods, where no one is actually that close, geographically, to each other) that get to know each other, and this is a great place for your child to make friends. I know it's not fun to drive your kid an hour just for a movie night, but it's crucial for their development, and everyone will be much happier!

For more information on alternative education, visit www.educationrevolution.org.

3. Security

This may not seem like a family or social consideration, but because it involves the safety and wellbeing of your loved ones, I feel that it's a good fit here. No matter how far out into the wilderness you go, there are going to be some other people around. They may live fifteen or twenty miles away, but they're still there. And you never know when a backpacker or two might come trudging by. For the most part, the people that you'll meet while you're living self-sufficiently will be pretty harmless; they're content living their own lives and leaving you to yours. However, security is still an important thing to take into consideration, especially if you're preparing for an apocalypse-level event. In that case, the resources that you've created and stockpiled will become very valuable. In a non apocalyptic setting, people are more worried about keeping animals out of their garden than they are trespassers off their land, but that counts as a kind of security too.

In general, most people are content with some level of fencing around the border of their land. Whether that's a small wire fence, an electric fence, or a stone wall is up to you and how much security you feel you need. In general, some barbed wire and clearly posted signs stating "This is private, occupied land" will be enough to convince people that your property isn't abandoned and isn't a good target for squatting. If you're interested in investing more time and money in a more significant security system, you can also add motion sensors and flood lights that will turn on when something larger than a dog or a coyote comes near the fence.

As for your house, it's a good idea to have sturdy locks on all of the doors and storage facilities to keep any wandering people or animals from getting too curious. Whether you want to provide enough electricity for an alarm system is up to you—it might be just as effective (and a lot more fun) to keep a dog or two. Certain large breeds, like German shepherds and huskies, make pretty good guard dogs, as they are very protective. Even a smaller dog, like a beagle or a shih tzu, can serve as an effective burglar alarm. Fortunately, making homemade dog food isn't too hard, so you won't be spending a lot of resources on your alternative alarm system.

Some people go as far as creating a panic room, which is a well-hidden, nigh impregnable room that contains a week or two's worth of food, toiletries, and everything else needed to survive for a time hiding out. You won't often find panic rooms on schematics, as they're meant to be totally secret and secure. It can be expensive to build an effective one, but if you're really interested in being completely secure, it's an option you should consider.

And, finally, I'll mention firearms. While I don't endorse the use of firearms against other people, a shot into the air can be a great way to scare an intruder (or a really large animal) off of your property. If you're going to be hunting, you'll likely have a rifle or a shotgun around anyway, so you can think of it as a double investment.

Some final notes

In the previous chapters, I've outlined a lot of information—what living off the grid is; how to procure land, housing, electricity, water, and food; how to be prepared for an emergency; and a few tips on managing your family and social lives when you're living self-sufficiently. It's a lot of information to cover in such a short book! But with the points I've set out, you should feel well-prepared to start planning your off-grid move and have a good idea of what it might be like to live away from civilization, depending only on yourself for survival (or at least having the ability to do so).

Before leaving you to your adventure, I'd like to make two final notes. First, be aware that there's a very large community of self-sufficiency enthusiasts out there, both online and in your state. Don't hesitate to get in contact with them to ask questions, get advice, and share stories. It's generally a welcoming community, and people are more than happy to share their experiences and help you out in your endeavors.

Second, be patient, and don't expect everything to go smoothly. Moving off the grid is a difficult process, and one that often takes a few years to totally adjust to. It's not for everyone, and many people have definitely gone back to living in society. There's nothing wrong with that, but sufficient planning and preparation are key to the success of any lifestyle change, self-sufficiency included. There are going to be times when it's really difficult, and there are likely to be people who aren't supportive. You may face some negativity from your family and friends, but everyone will adjust to the idea, and life will go back to normal after a while. When it gets tough, just take a deep breath, remind yourself why you're doing it, and know that things do get easier.

I wish you the best of luck with your off-grid living. Maybe I'll see you out there!

Books by Jim Kilpatrick

Beginner's Backyard Chickens

Survive and Thrive

Simple Food Storage Strategies

www.amazon.com/author/jimkilpatrick

About Jim Kilpatrick

Jim Kilpatrick is a structural engineer, "backyard farmer" and breeder of prize roses.

After completing a degree in structural engineering at the University of Pennsylvania, Jim entered the world of consulting. Always looking for a way to add more quality to life; he has started raising his own chickens. "Only after you've tasted the difference between store-bought eggs and home-produced ones, will you appreciate the difference in quality. There's just no comparison really." he says.

Jim also enjoys growing his family's own herbs and vegetables. He is a member of his local garden club and often gives talks and workshops on self-sufficiency. Recently he has started a local action group on the subject of bringing quality into the home in various ways. He is passionate about getting families involved in daily beneficial activities, and freely shares his knowledge with those interested in regaining the lost arts of producing quality home-grown food.

He believes in doing what you can to improve your life, but to also take things easy!

Jim lives in California with his wife, two teenagers, a flock of chickens and a very lazy Dachshund.

One Last Thing...

Thank you so much for reading my book. I hope you really liked it. As you probably know, many people look at the reviews before they decide to purchase a book. If you liked the book, could you please take a minute to leave a review with your feedback? 60 seconds is all I'm asking for, and it would mean the world to me.

Jim Kilpatrick

Images and Cover by Traditionally Modern Publishers

TRADITIONALLY
MODERN

Atlanta, Georgia USA

32103598R00037

Made in the USA
Lexington, KY
07 May 2014